Vilissa Thomp

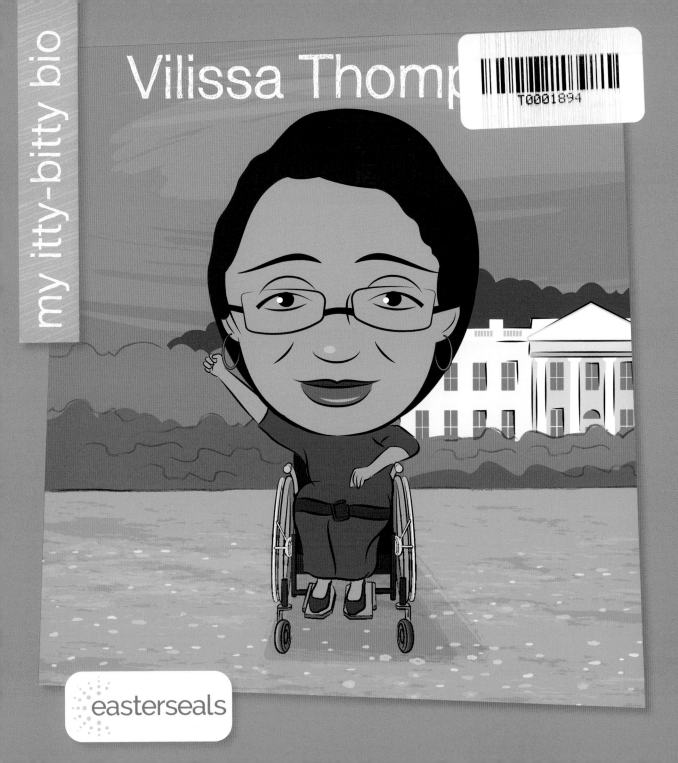

easterseals

CHERRY LAKE PRESS

Published in the United States of America by Cherry Lake Publishing Group
Ann Arbor, Michigan
www.cherrylakepublishing.com

Reading Adviser: Beth Walker Gambro, MS, Ed., Reading Consultant, Yorkville, IL
Book Designer: Jennifer Wahi
Illustrator: Jeff Bane

Photo Credits: © Vilissa Thompson, 5, 9, 17, 21; © LuYago/Shutterstock, 7; © Vitalii Vodolazskyi/Shutterstock, 11; © Billion Photos/Shutterstock, 13, 22; © Clemson University, 15; © C-SPAN, 19, 23

Cherry Lake Press is an imprint of Cherry Lake Publishing Group.

Library of Congress Cataloging-in-Publication Data

Names: Evans, Nicole (Nicole Lynn) author. | Bane, Jeff, 1957- illustrator.

Title: Vilissa Thompson / by Nicole Evans, Jeff Bane.
Description: Ann Arbor, Michigan : Cherry Lake Publishing, [2023] | Series: My itty-bitty bio | Audience: Grades K-1 | Summary: "Meet Vilissa Thompson, an advocate for disabled people, especially disabled women of color, in this biography for early readers. This book examines her life and impact in a simple, age-appropriate way that helps young readers develop word recognition and reading skills. The My Itty-Bitty Bio series celebrates diversity, covering women and men from a range of backgrounds and professions including immigrants and individuals with disabilities"-- Provided by publisher.
Identifiers: LCCN 2023009115 | ISBN 9781668927274 (hardcover) | ISBN 9781668928325 (paperback) | ISBN 9781668929797 (ebook) | ISBN 9781668931271 (pdf)
Subjects: LCSH: Thompson, Vilissa, 1985- | African Americans with disabilities--Biography--Juvenile literature. | African American women--Biography--Juvenile literature. | People with disabilities--United States--Social conditions--Juvenile literature.
Classification: LCC HV1569.3.A35 E83 2023 | DDC 362.4/08996073--dc23/eng/20230417
LC record available at https://lccn.loc.gov/2023009115

Printed in the United States of America
Corporate Graphics

The author would like to extend special thanks to Vilissa Thompson for her time and participation in the development of this book.

About the author: Nicole Evans is an actress, writer, and disability rights and inclusion activist. Born with osteogenesis imperfecta, Nicole is a full-time wheelchair user. She enjoys helping children with disabilities explore their identity and realize their full potential. Nicole lives in Los Angeles, California.

About the illustrator: Jeff Bane and his two business partners own a studio along the American River in Folsom, California, home of the 1849 Gold Rush. When Jeff's not sketching or illustrating for clients, he's either swimming or kayaking in the river to relax.

About our partnership: This title was developed in partnership with Easterseals to support its mission of empowering people with disabilities. Through their national network of affiliates, Easterseals provides essential services and on-the-ground supports to more than 1.5 million people each year.

I was born in 1985. I was born in Winnsboro, South Carolina.

I am a Black woman. I am disabled. I am **proud**.

Where do you live?

My disability is **rare**. It affects my bones.

It is called **osteogenesis imperfecta**.

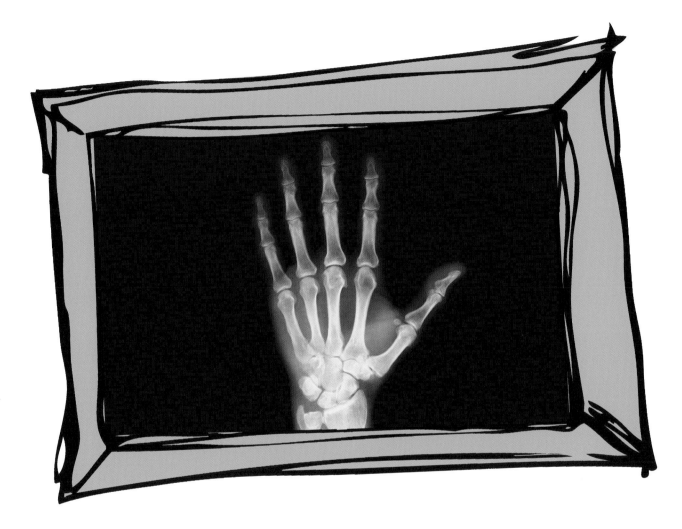

My bones break easily. I use a wheelchair. It is **manual**.

I went to school. I was top of my class. The Americans with Disabilities Act protected me.

Where do you go to school?

I went to college. I got a master's degree. I became a **social worker**.

I started a company. It is called Ramp Your Voice!

I use my voice. I speak out.
I fight for **inclusion**.

I spoke at the **Democratic National Convention** in 2020.

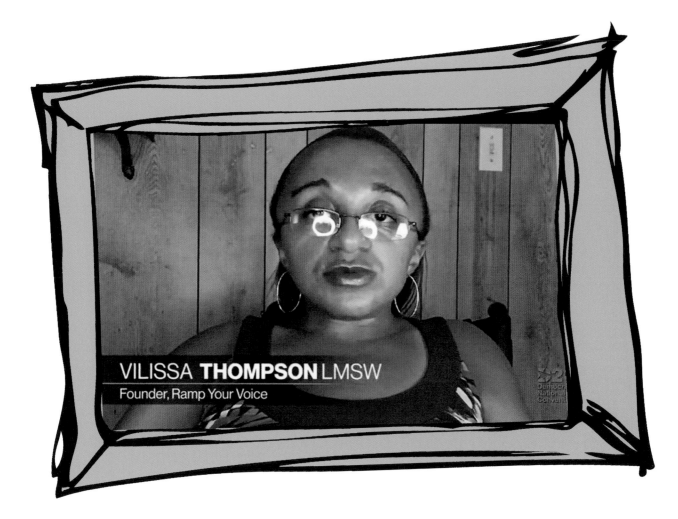

VILISSA **THOMPSON** LMSW
Founder, Ramp Your Voice

I am a writer. I share stores. I teach people. They learn. They make changes. I make a difference.

What would you like to ask me?

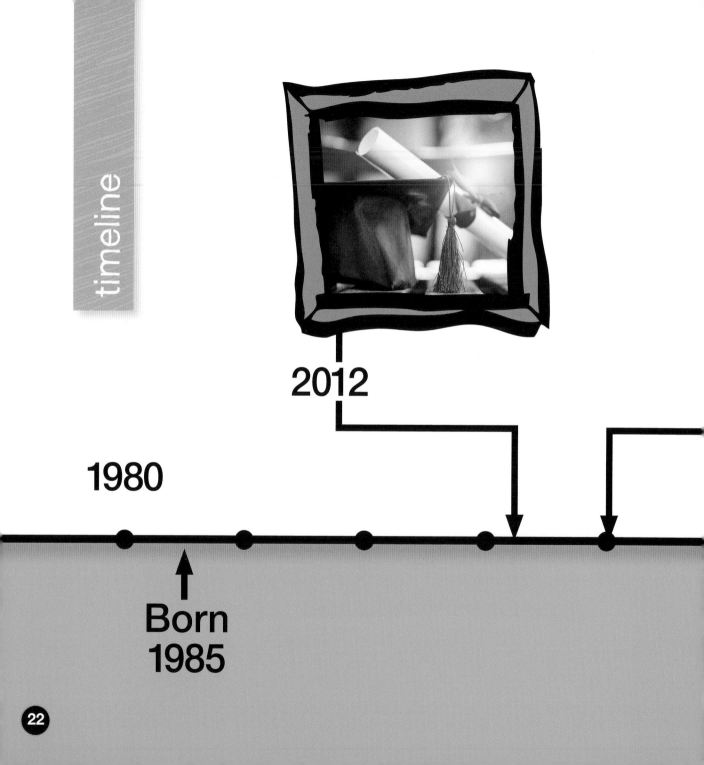

2012

1980

Born
1985

VILISSA **THOMPSON** LMSW
Founder, Ramp Your Voice

2020

2080

23

glossary

Democratic National Convention (DEM-uh-crat-ic NA-shun-uhl cuhn-VEN-shuhn) large political convention where a president is nominated every four years

inclusion (in-CLOO-zhuhn) the act of making sure everyone can participate

manual (MAN-yoo-uhl) operated by hand; without a motor

osteogenesis imperfecta (OST-ee-oh-jen-uh-sis IM-per-fec-ta) a rare disability characterized by bones that break easily

proud (PROWD) feeling pleased, satisfied, and worthy

rare (RAIR) not common

social worker (SOH-shuhl WERK-er) a person trained to help people work through challenges they face in everyday life

index